Nelsonville
from
A to Z

A publication of Stuart's Opera House Arts Education Program

Edited by Celeste Parsons
Illustrated by Hannah Sickles

This book is dedicated to all the talented people of Nelsonville, Ohio, and to those who encourage them.

ISBN   978-0-578-57177-5

Monday Creek Publishing LLC
mondaycreekpublishing.com

A is for Appalachian Ohio.

We treasure the hills, hollers, and people that surround us.

Where the landscape is constantly changing.
Going up and down.
From curve to curve.
The green view for half the year.
The vibrant colors for a quarter.
For the animals who roam the vast acreage,
The large predators to the small prey,
For the large eagle watching the small hare,
Appalachia is large and grand.
Appalachia has provided us refuge.
Appalachia is home.

Andrew Benjamin Brunton

B is for Bricks.

Bricks made in Nelsonville include Nelsonville Block and Star Brick pavers, used for sidewalks and streets in town and shipped all over the Midwest.

Snowflake Brick

Star Brick

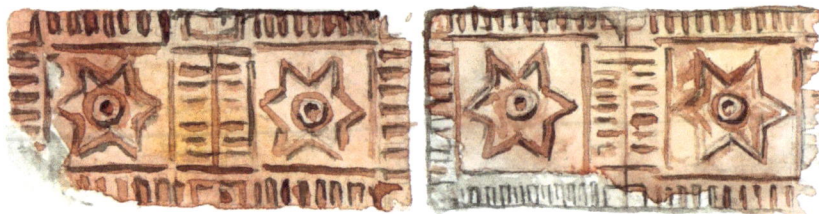

The streets glitter with the shining Star Bricks
Six points make the star
The rough and grainy texture makes your hands tingle
The ever more shining star is a sure reminder of happiness
You will never fail to realize where you are
Follow the Star Brick road and you will end up back home
Shining Star Bricks may be dull
But as if bright suns they light up Nelsonville
Stars provide hope and comfort
Bricks build the foundation of a home
Star Bricks show you are home and welcome
Always offering a way to go home

Nevaeh Gonzalez

C is for Canal.

The Hocking Canal, completed in 1843, linked Athens, Chauncey, Nelsonville, and Logan to Lancaster, and ran through town where Canal Street is now.

Canals once were handmade
creating swirling currents
rushing down to carry wealth over 56 miles,
now paved as the core of the town
with hard cement
to have cars carry the wealth through the town.

Mary Ellen Hoobler

D is for Dew House.

Thomas Dew built the Dew House in 1830 as a hotel and tavern. Theodore Roosevelt spoke from the porch in 1912 when he was campaigning for president.

What will you do when you do at the Dew?
Open up a hotel with a Public Square view
And a tavern below to serve whiskey and wine
In 1839.
What will you do to improve at the Dew?
Add on a porch and a third story, too,
Making both outdoors and indoors look great
In 1878.
What do you find when you stay at the Dew?
You hire a room for one dollar or two,
And use the first phone line to Poston Livery
In 1903.
What will you see on the porch of the Dew?
In nineteen and twelve, when Ted Roosevelt comes through,
You might climb a phone pole, if you're rather small,
To witness it all.
What will you do at the Dew House today?
Rent an apartment, dine at a cafe.
The Dew is alive at the edge of the Square -
So come meet me there.

Celeste Parsons

E is for Education.

Daniel Nelson, who founded Nelsonville in 1818, donated the lot for the first school, which was completed in 1856.

The bell rings.
I hear education calling -
        Or, at least, my school day -
Agonizing, memorizing,
Looking for the inspiration,
        And, at last, release.
The bell rings.
What does education cost me?
        Is it worth my spending
Anxious effort and frustrations,
Costs laid out on expectations,
        Discipline unending?
The bell rings.
Where will education lead me,
        Today or tomorrow?
Overwhelming or empowering,
Passion, hope, or exploration
        Mine to seize or borrow.
Education.
Daniel thought it fundamental,
        Donating the land -
Worth the struggle for the power,
Revolution, but unequal -
        Both an "or" and "and."

Celeste Parsons

F is for Fountain.

The iron fountain in the center of the Public Square was built in 1904.

I wonder why
    they call it a fountain.
It doesn't spout
    like most fountains do,
But the water drips
    and drizzles and dribbles
And bubbles and burbles
    And splashes and spills
Till it finally trickles
    Into a pool
Where it ripples and wavers
    Clear and cool
With wishes
    For fishes.

Celeste Parsons

G is for Good Vibrations.

Whether it's one of the 60+ bands playing at the Nelsonville Music Fest, or someone playing on his own front porch, music is all around.

Mountain music all around
Brass strings and bells fill the room with sound
Drinking spirits and lifting them too
There's nothing that a good band can't do

Ma and Pa out on the porch
Playing the blues by light of the torch
Good vibrations are sent through our soul
The sound of music making our hearts full

No matter where the music takes us
It truly is what makes us

Nicole Clonch

H is for Hocking River.

The Hocking River runs past Nelsonville on its way to the Ohio River. It is too shallow for large boats, but perfect for canoes and kayaks.

The Hocking
is a winding river
beside tall trees and rustling leaves -
shallow rivulets and yearly turbulence.
Old trains settle a few steps away -
A pink and white passenger car
in the midst of rusty locomotives.
Bicycle riders spin close to the river
near the once clamorous trains.
A veil of snow falls on the water -
peace comes eerie and lonesome.
I walk past an old house with broken
curlicue fences. Sixteen windows face
the Hocking River - the same river once
rushed by that house, paint fresh
with faith and aspirations. Time-worn
stones remember dry creeks
and flash floods spread onto streets.
You have to love the river - enough
to brave disasters, enough to stay.

Robin Schaffer

I is for Initial Rocks.

Generations of Nelsonville young people carved their initials into these boulders, located northeast of town.

Initial: the first letter found in a
Name, an appellation, an
Identity. One person,
Two names, two letters,
Incised, and precise,
Anticipating, not closing, a
Life.

Rocks: the first layer, supporting the hills,
Overlooking the valley, with leaves overlain.
Carvings, now moss-blurred, marking occasions:
Kisses, promises, and celebrations.
Stones have long memories.

Celeste Parsons

J is for John Hunt Morgan.

Confederate General John Hunt Morgan passed through Nelsonville on July 22, 1863. He took fresh horses and asked local women to feed his men supper, but spared canal boats from burning.

John Hunt Morgan, he came riding
Out of the green Kentucky hills
Over the river to Indiana
 Bringing the war up north.

John Hunt Morgan, he came riding
Into Ohio, to Buffington Isle,
Met stiff resistance from Union soldiers
 Lost seven hundred men.

John Hunt Morgan, he came riding,
Fleeing eastward to Nelsonville.
Horses were tired, soldiers were hungry:
 They made the housewives cook.

John Hunt Morgan, he left riding,
Union soldiers hot on his tail.
Captured before he could get to Kentucky
 Brought to Columbus jail.

John Hunt Morgan and six officers
Dug a tunnel under the wall,
Found a skiff and crossed the Ohio
 Home for the end of the war.

John Hunt Morgan, he came riding. . . .

Celeste Parsons

K is for Kilns.

A kiln is a large furnace where bricks were baked. The ruined kilns of the Nelsonville Brick Company, which closed in 1937, are on Rt. 278 (near the city offices).

 They look like little homes
For gnomes
Or elves
Or even for we ourselves

No windows, though
No light
Better for creatures of the night
Bats, feral cats, or rats

Once fiery hellzapoppin bakers of bricks inside
Now only the tired stink of dank, rank coal ash resides

But still
I remain enchanted.

Amy Abercrombie

L is for Lock.

A lock was a little piece of a canal with a gate at each end. By "locking" the gates around a canal boat and then letting water in or out, the boat could be raised or lowered. Lock 19 of the Hocking Canal is just north of Nelsonville, but the gates are long gone.

Locks usually shut things out,
Enclose, retain.
Canal locks let things pass,
Lift up, move on.

The gates, now missing, closed
The ends. The boats
Inside the narrow space
Rose up, or fell.

The water traveled one way;
Either way, boats.
A contradiction, this -
Or so it seems.

The walls still stand, but hold
Waves of grasses -
In or out, no boat passes
Except in dreams.

Celeste Parsons

M is for Mine.

The mines all around made Nelsonville the largest town in the area in the late 19th and early 20th centuries. Men mined both coal and clay.

M is for the mines
For the endless hours
For the struggle to make a living
The unappreciated sacrifice
History built on the backs of men who go unknown
Men who delved into the depths of the earth to care for their families
Children who hung their heads in shame at their father's job
Men who came home covered in soot and dirt
Drinking away their salaries
Signing their lives away to a company
Profits made by men who did no work
Men who took and never gave
Men who gave it all and took nothing
M is for the mines
For the history that runs through our veins
Like the endless tunnels below our feet

Kenzie Winchell

N is for Nelson House.

Originally built on the southwest corner of the Public Square in 1814 by town founder Daniel Nelson, this house has been moved three times.

I don't look it, if I say so myself,
But I go way back.
I wear modern trappings
But underneath
It's the same old me
Doing the same old job:
Holding a family safe,
Keeping them warm,
Being their space.
Well, not the same space.
I've had to pack up
And move
Three times
And downsize, too -
Cut my middle right out!
These grounds are not as large
As those I first had
On the Square.
What we do
To survive!

Celeste Parsons

O is for Outdoor Art.

A building wall doesn't just hold up the roof.

O is for Outdoor Art
Where creativity is shown.
Beauty fills these empty streets.
People witness the minds of others
While never even meeting them.
Accomplishments sown and
Evolution marked on the land.
Feelings portrayed for the public to see.
O is for Outdoor Art.

Isaac W. Hull

This mural appears on the back of the First National Bank. Look for the street scenes at the Post Office parking lot and the parking lot across from the Elks Club, the mountain mural at the Rocky Brands outlet, the giant star bricks on Canal Street, the tower of bricks at Robbins Crossing, and the book and quotations at the park next to the library.

P is for Public Square.

The land donated by Daniel Nelson in 1823 quickly became the focus of business and social gatherings.

Public space, our
Place, everyone's front lawn,

Where we huddle under midnight skies
Mute with grief
As flames and smoke
Erupt from windows,
Then cheer water spouting
From fire hoses;

Where we gather
Winding between carnie trailers,
Jumping over cables,
Rushing from ride to ride;
Where pageant queens of all ages
Wave solemnly from convertibles
As the parade passes.

Consolations, celebrations,
Merging with the air
We breathe. The
Center, the town's heart.

Celeste Parsons

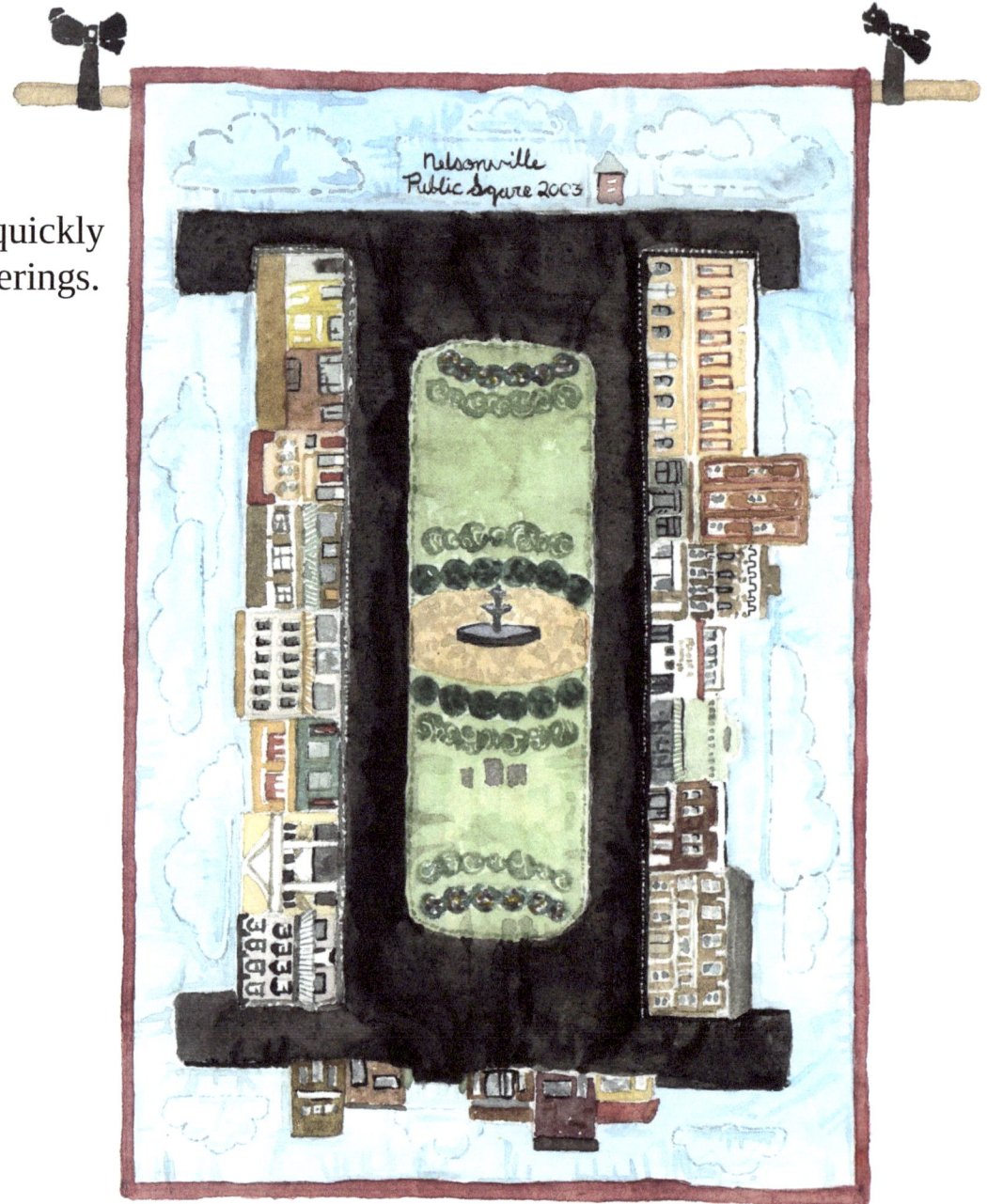

This quilt shows the Public Square as it was in 2003. The back side of the quilt is signed by representatives of each business shown.

Q is for Quandary.

A Quandary is what you are in when you don't know what to do.

I'm sure it happens to everyone
Who's writing an alphabet book. It's fun
As you breeze along through A, B, C
With lots of choice in vocabulary.
But then you run up against Q -
And what do you do?

Oh, there *are* words for Q, like "Quaint,"
But unique to Nelsonville it ain't.
And how would you illustrate it?
I Quit.

Celeste Parsons

R is for Railroad.

Railroad reliability put an end to the canals, which needed lots of maintenance to repair frequent flood damage. Now the Hocking Scenic Railway gives tour rides on the rails that once carried freight.

Up and down
Side to side
Left to ride
Forward and backward
Rusty tracks leading
from to and fro
Following the beat
Of its own drum
Whistleblowing
Take a ride
Over town
anywhere you need
Follow your dreams
Follow the train

Sophitia Anderson

S is for Stuart's Opera House.

Hear a band, see a play, hold a wedding, take music lessons - it's all been happening at Stuart's since 1879.

The Opera House is haunted, some will say,
By spiteful spirits, fond of playing pranks:
The sound cues in their console rearranged;
A light found on when it had been turned off
(Or off, when it was on); a whispered sound
Of footsteps pacing down an empty hall
To lift hair off your neck. The ghosts I've met
Are friendlier: a title, and a trace
Of smile upon a poster charred almost
To ash, still glued to brick; the fading wisp
Of song caught up within a curtain fold
Left by a child performing his first role;
A throbbing floorboard like feet beating time
To fiddle tunes; the faint echo of hands
Applauding youths in graduation gowns;
The hush of held breath staving off the tears
Of joy, or grief, or wonder; or a shape
Caught in the dust motes swirling in the glow
Of "ghost lamp" left alight in darkened hall
Awaiting the next show.

Celeste Parsons

T is for Trails.

Trails for walking, biking, or off-road vehicles are all found nearby.

There is, in my hometown of Marietta, a street named Sacra Via.
It's a Latin phrase that means *Sacred Way*.
I found my own Sacra Via - my own sacred way - unrolling through
Wayne National Forest, stretching over 13 miles to Athens.
A very short walk from Public Square, and I am walking along the
Hockhocking Adena Bikeway, the soles of my feet pounding the same
Path as many trains did in the centuries before. Nelsonville behind me,
The asphalt trail is my path.
The tall trees, the high rocks, and the canopy of blue sky above all of it
Makes me think. All I need are shoes, a clear sky, and the mileposts
By the side of the road marking my progress a half mile at a time.
This is where my thoughts and my dreams are the only company I need.
It's the length of a half marathon, but there are no cheering spectators,
No volunteers passing me cups of water and Gatorade, and there won't be
A medal that I can hang on the wall above my desk. But what I <u>do</u> win
Are hours on this trail, with the Hocking River faithfully by my side.
I would tell a person who would eschew the confines of a house of worship
To step onto the Hockhocking Adena Bikeway and be open to the sacred.
It is a place where you are both alone and with everything at the same time,
In a leaf-shaded, twig-floored temple without walls.

Paul T. Evans

U is for Underwater.

Every now and then, the Hocking River overflows, as it did in 1907.

Our street is like a river wild
The sticks and debris float by
You should have moved your car out of the flow
But you didn't know

My son took out his fishing pole
Thought he would catch a bite
Turned out he hooked something in the road
How would he ever know

The neighbors are all standing by
This never happened before
We laugh, we sigh, we wonder why
Perhaps we'll never know

Jennifer L'Heureux

V is for Vitalize.

It's a new sidewalk, new city, built on the past.

Little town   built on coal:
Underground   mine cars roll.
Overground   bricks are made.
Some folks left,   some folks stayed.

Canal boats   come and go;
Railroad comes -   not as slow.
Opera house   brings in shows.
Little town   thrives and grows,

Coal runs out.   Mines shut down.
Hard times come   on the town.
Jobs are few: "Store for rent."
Some folks stayed,   some folks went.

Artists move   into place,
Clean and paint   vacant space.
Fires burn;   folks build back.
New trains run   down the track.

Turning old   into new -
Visitors   like it, too.
Town still has   much to give.
Vitalize: make it live.

Celeste Parsons

 **is for Wildflowers.**

In the woods, meadows, or along roads, seasons are marked by the changing blooms.

Wildflower meadows
small delicate pods of dull white
exploding - wide, flat,
and clustered with small flowers,
Queen Anne's Lace.
Creamy yellow and white flowers
abundant with butterflies and bees,
smells of early spring and sunshine,
honeysuckle.

    Mary Ellen Hoobler

Large White Trillium

Bluebells

Phlox

Large-flowered
Bellwort

Dutchman's Britches

Blue-eyed Mary

Toadshade
(Sessile Trillium)

Dandelion

X is for Robbins Xing.

Visit this collection of log cabins on the Hocking College campus to see what life was like in the 1850s.

Each time I enter a restored log cabin at Robbins Crossing
I am awash in nostalgia
A feeling of coming home
I seem to belong there
A cozy fire blazing warmth
Confirms it

So, is there reincarnation after all?
And do you get that same feeling?
Let me know . . . .

Amy Abercrombie

Y is for Yesterday.

History lingers in the quiet grounds of Fort Street Cemetery, where headstones recall founder Daniel Nelson and Civil War soldiers.

Black limbs cracked, broken, fall
scattered over
brown leaves' mats and dew
where summers made visits with roses, where new grasses trickled with violets
where winds made winters, springtimes came to change
You stood firm
I laid to rest
Once friends crowned my head in lilies
Now strangers come only to question,
Ah, there are stories . . .
et tu Brute?
Your roots, then strong as talons, held my jewelry box upon the hill
but now are sinking waters, our woods rotted, folding inward,
stones' etchings gone with mosses
not long are we remembered
Yet your head still hails the sky and pulls my spirit with you
we grasp at light, becoming vapors
What would be dust's left at the gate,
but there are clouds above the meadow.

Sandra Russell

Z is for Zigzag.

Whether you are traveling on road or water, your route will wind through our hills!

A garter snake zigzags its way through the leaves.

Where did it come from?
Where is it going?
Hard to say,
Hard to see.

Curving and bending,
Climbing and falling,
I'm in the middle.
I'm in the now.

Beginning lost,
End unseen
Appalachian life
In between.

Celeste Parsons

LIST OF CONTRIBUTORS

Amy Abercrombie: "K is for Kilns"; "X is for Robbins Xing"

Sophitia Anderson (Nelsonville-York High School): "R is for Railroad"

Andrew Benjamin Brunton (Tri-County Career Center): "A is for Appalachian Ohio"

Nicole Clonch (Tri-County Career Center): "G is for Good Vibrations"

Paul T. Evans: "T Is for Trails"

Nevaeh Gonzalez (Nelsonville-York High School): "B is for Bricks"

Mary Ellen Hoobler (Nelsonville-York High School): "C is for Canal"; "W is for Wildflowers"

Isaac W. Hull (Tri-County Career Center): "O is for Outdoor Art"

Jennifer Tvorik L'Heureux: "U Is for Underwater"

Celeste Parsons: "D is for Dew House"; "E is for Education"; "F is for Fountain"; "I is for Initial Rocks"; "J is for John Hunt Morgan"; "L is for Lock"; "N is for Nelson House"; "P is for Public Square"; "Q is for Quandary"; "S is for Stuart's Opera House"; "V is for Vitalize"; "Z is for Zigzag"

Sandra Russell: "Y is for Yesterday"

Robin Schaffer, "H is for Hocking River"

Kenzie Winchell (Tri-County Career Center): "M is for Mine"

Stuart's Opera House, Nelsonville, Ohio

The purpose of Stuart's Opera House is to celebrate music, promote our region's local assets, and create an environment where community is cultivated through the performing arts. We fulfill this purpose when we engage in activities that also support our mission to be a regional leader in the arts community, a center for public expression, and an economic development partner for Southeastern Ohio.

Our Arts Education Program furthers our mission by providing much needed art education and inspiration to our region. We offer an affordable, broad-based program focused on performing arts. The special events, afterschool, day-time classes, and summer programs allow for Arts Education that reaches Southeast Ohio residents of most ages and backgrounds. The overarching outcome of our program is diverse participation where community identity can be freely and openly expressed. Our program is designed to be flexible and responsive to community needs.

Under the branch of Stuart's Art Education Program we offer: theater performances for primary students; an afterschool music program; a visiting artist and artist-in-residence program; a drama club and production for Nelsonville-York High School; a creative writing program for adults; regional coordination for the national Poetry Out Loud competition; private music lessons for children ages 6-18; an Appalachian Music Program in partnership with Athens County Public Libraries; and free admission to all children under 12 to the Nelsonville Music Festival.

Our education programs received 2019 funding from Epstein-Teicher Philanthropies, the Ohio Arts Council, The People's Bank Foundation, The Charles G O'Bleness Foundation, the Athens County Foundation, The Johnny B and John Spataro Fund, Benefest, The Athens Community Music Festival, ETC, Kleinpenny Education Fund, and several individuals and local businesses.

About the Editor

Celeste Parsons lives outside of Nelsonville in a log house built on a former dairy farm, with her husband Jim, her Westie dog Spook, and a revolving population of deer, turkeys, chipmunks, hummingbirds, and other wildlife. She enjoys gardening, anything having to do with fabric or thread, reading, and bicycle touring with Jim on their tandem bike (64,000 miles since the year 2000, and counting). She is also an enthusiastic member of the ABC Players and thinks of Stuart's Opera House as her second home. She has written poems, plays, technical documentation, and newspaper articles since childhood. This is her first published book.

About the Illustrator

Hannah Sickles was raised in Athens, Ohio, alongside her twin sister. She has learned most of what she knows from her mother, who spent years studying fine art. Still residing in the foothills of Appalachia, Hannah has her own business working with watercolors, and creating copper enamel jewelry. Besides illustrating and enameling, Hannah can be found making theater magic with ABC Players, or maybe playing yard golf in Zaleski forest. Hannah finds inspiration from nature, her two orange cats, and a group of amazing friends.

www.ingramcontent.com/pod-product-compliance
Lightning Source LLC
Chambersburg PA
CBHW042106090426

42811CB00018B/1870